Guide to Mortgage Lending in Indian Country

Table of Contents

1

Overview

This Guide to Mortgage Lending in Indian Country provides banks with an introduction to issues frequently encountered when making mortgage loans to Native Americans. It is intended to highlight the most important of these issues while also providing information about other resources available to bankers interested in learning more about lending in Indian country.

The guide is divided into four sections. Part I — Operating in Indian Country provides background information about legal issues involving Native Americans and Indian land. Part II — Residential Mortgage Lending Process highlights steps in the mortgage lending process unique to Indian country. Part III — Types of Mortgage Loan Programs describes various government loan guarantee and secondary market programs available to lenders doing business with Native Americans. And finally, Part IV — Compliance Issues addresses issues prevalent in mortgage lending on an Indian reservation. The guide also includes seven appendixes listing regional offices of relevant organizations and government agencies.

PLEASE NOTE: This guide is intended to provide only an introduction to mortgage lending in Indian country. National banks should not rely on it as legal advice. To answer legal questions, banks should consult with local counsel familiar with federal Indian law and the laws of the tribes in their communities. For technical assistance about the Bureau of Indian Affairs' (BIA) approval process, banks should contact the BIA. Section III of this guide presents general summaries of loan programs but does not include detailed information about the requirements of the programs. For more information about a particular program, banks should contact the agency that administers it.

Part I — Operating in Indian Country

When a bank introduces a new product, enters a new line of business, or expands its customer base, it should first get to know its market. Doing business in Indian country is no exception. In order to offer successfully mortgage products to Native Americans residing on reservations, a bank must invest time in building relationships with tribal governments.

In the United States, there are more than 500 federally recognized Indian tribes, including more than 200 Alaska Native villages. Indian tribes are governments — most have their own laws, including foreclosure and leasing ordinances, and their own justice systems to enforce tribal law. While mortgage lenders will encounter many of the same issues across Indian country, each reservation may present a unique set of circumstances. Bankers can enhance their marketing efforts by taking the time to get to know a tribe's laws and relevant customs and protocols.

The best way for a bank to learn more about a particular tribe is to contact the tribal government directly. The structure of tribal governments varies depending on the size of the tribe, but banks can contact the tribal chairman or president's office to set up an initial meeting.

For assistance in determining whom to contact, national banks can consult with OCC's community reinvestment development specialists headquartered in each of OCC's district offices. The specialists' names and phone numbers are listed in the appendix A of this guide. Banks may also contact the Community Development Division in Washington, D.C. at (202) 874-4930.

Lenders must recognize that Indian culture will shape the manner in which tribes and tribal members relate to the bank. To educate bankers about Indian culture, this guide offers general information about Native Americans, tribes, Indian land, and tribal sovereignty.

Who is an Indian or a Native American? Although many Indian people use the term "Indian," some prefer "Native American," or their own tribal affiliation, such as "Lakota," "Mohawk," or "Navajo." Since this is a general guide, it uses the terms "Native American" and "Indian" interchangeably. To be regarded as an Indian or Alaska Native for most governmental and jurisdictional purposes, a person must generally: (1) be of Indian descent; and (2) be an enrolled member of a federally recognized Indian tribe.

What is an Indian tribe? The United States has a unique legal and government-to-government relationship with Indian tribes reflected in the Constitution of the United States, treaties, statutes, and court decisions. The Supreme Court has described Indian tribes as "domestic dependent nations"[1] with governmental authority over their members and their territory. Under federal law, the Secretary of the Interior maintains a list of Indian tribes that are recognized by the United States as governments.[2]

What is Indian country? The definition of "Indian country" has changed over history, but the term generally is used today to describe collectively Indian territory throughout the United States. Congress has defined "Indian country" as land inside the boundaries of Indian reservations, communities made up mainly of Indians, and Indian trust and restricted land.[3]

What is Indian land? "Indian land" is any restricted or trust land, even if such land stands outside of reservation boundaries. "Trust land" means land the title to which is held in trust by the United States for an individual Indian or a tribe.[4] "Restricted land" means land the title to which is held by an individual Indian or a tribe and which can only be alienated or encumbered by the owner with the approval of the Secretary of the Interior because of limitations contained in the conveyance instrument pursuant to federal law or because of a federal law directly imposing such limitations.[5]

Land ownership on Indian reservations includes individual trust or restricted land, tribal trust land, and fee simple land, each of which presents different issues for lenders. Reservations that are a mosaic of Indian and non-Indian owned land are sometimes referred to as "checker board" reservations.

- Individually owned lands are of two kinds:

    (1)   Trust land — The federal government holds legal title but the beneficial interest remains with the individual Indian.

    (2)   Restricted fee land — An individual Indian holds legal title but with legal restrictions against alienation or encumbrance.

---

[1] Cherokee Nation v. Georgia, 30 U.S. (5 Pet.) 1, 17 (1831).

[2] 61 Fed. Reg. 58,211-02 (1996). This list is posted on BIA's website at http://www.doi.gov/bureau-indian-affairs.html.

[3] 18 USC § 1151.

[4] 25 CFR § 151.2(d).

[5] 25 CFR § 151.2(e).

- Tribally owned lands are of three kinds:

  (1)   Trust land — The federal government holds legal title but the beneficial interest remains with the tribe.
  (2)   Restricted fee land — The tribe holds legal title but with legal restrictions against alienation or encumbrance.
  (3)   Fee land purchased by tribes — The tribe acquires legal title under specific statutory authority. However, by operation of law, the title becomes restricted because, without the consent of Congress, it cannot be alienated and, without the consent of the Secretary of Interior, it cannot be encumbered.

- Fee simple land

  (1)   Some reservations include fee simple land — that is, land whose title is held absolutely by the owner, without restriction, in the same way that lands are generally held throughout the United States.

Can banks make mortgage loans on Indian land? Yes, under certain circumstances. Generally, banks secure mortgage loans with ownership or leasehold interests in real property. In Indian country, the United States often holds the title to land in trust for an Indian tribe or an individual Indian, and such lands are referred to as trust lands. Tribal trust lands may be leased in accordance with federal law, but may not be mortgaged or sold. Lenders may obtain mortgages with ownership or leasehold interests in real estate as security for loans involving individual Indian trust lands in accordance with federal law. Because federal law treats tribal and individual trust lands differently, a bank must know the status of the land in order to determine how it can obtain a security interest.

Individual trust or restricted land

Real property held in trust or restricted status by the federal government for individual tribal members may be mortgaged with the approval of the Secretary of the Interior, and may be subject to lien and foreclosure.[6] In 1956, Congress explicitly authorized mortgages and foreclosures of individual allotments[7]

> "to encourage individual Indian landholders to utilize commercial credit to the maximum extent possible," to encourage the extension of that credit by

---

[6] 25 USC § 483a.

[7] An "allotment" is land that was removed from tribal ownership and given to individual members of the tribe by the federal government during the late nineteenth and twentieth centuries. Today, this land is generally held by the descendants of the "allottee" as individual trust or restricted land.

reassuring lenders that they could obtain foreclosurable first mortgages on trust lands, and to clarify that the federal government would not be a necessary party or retain any claim to the land after a foreclosure sale.[8]

The law clearly states that individual trust or restricted land can be mortgaged, and, with the consent of the Secretary of the Interior, can be sold to a person who is not a member of the tribe if foreclosure is inevitable or the property cannot be transferred within the tribe. The non-tribal member would receive a fee simple interest in the land. To obtain the Secretary's consent, a bank must gain the approval of the BIA, a process described in part II of this guide.

However, Native Americans with individual trust or restricted lands may be reluctant to mortgage their land because, in the event of foreclosure, the land leaves its trust or restricted status and could leave Indian ownership. In order to avoid this problem, a holder of individual or restricted trust land may prefer to use a leasehold interest as collateral instead of the land itself. Using a leasehold interest as collateral for a mortgage also requires Secretarial approval, as described below in the "Tribal trust land" section.

Individual trust or restricted land is often conveyed to the descendants of allottees. The number of undivided interests in the resulting tenancy in common may sometimes make it difficult for lenders to negotiate a mortgage. For more information on how to overcome problems of "fractionalization," banks should contact the tribe or nearest BIA area office. A list of the BIA area offices is included in appendix B of this guide.

Tribal trust land

Because federal law generally prohibits a lender from obtaining a mortgage on real property held in trust by the federal government for an Indian tribe,[9] tribal trust and restricted lands present the greatest challenge to extending credit. But these legal barriers are not insurmountable. Loans secured by leasehold interests in tribal trust or restricted lands are permissible.

Where a tribe has developed a program in which it executes a lease as a lessor, an individual can offer as collateral a leasehold interest in either tribal or individual trust or restricted land, subject to approval of the BIA.[10] While some tribes are authorized by

---

[8] Northwest S.D. Prod. Credit Ass'n v. Smith, 784 F.2d 323, 326 (8th Cir. 1986), quoting S. Rep. No. 1647, 84th Cong., 2d Sess., reprinted in 1956 U.S.C.C.A.N. 2304-05.

[9] 25 USC § 177.

[10] 25 USC § 415(a) and 25 CFR part 162.

Congress to enter into 99-year leases, most can offer 50-year residential leases.[11] Banks can learn about leasing programs available on reservations in their communities by contacting the tribal government or the nearest BIA area office.

Fee simple land

Fee simple land owned by an individual within the boundaries of an Indian reservation does not carry the same restrictions as trust or restricted land and can be readily mortgaged. However, the use of fee simple land is still subject to the tribal sovereignty issues discussed below. Making loans secured by an interest in fee simple land owned by a tribe does require BIA approval.

What is tribal sovereignty? Before the Europeans settled in America, Indian tribes were sovereign political communities. Since the formation of the United States, the federal government has recognized Indian tribes as domestic dependent nations under its protection. The Constitution recognizes the sovereign status of Indian tribes by classing Indian treaties among the "supreme law of the land" and establishes Indian affairs as a uniquely federal area of concern. As domestic dependent nations, federally recognized Indian tribes, including Alaska Native Villages, possess power to govern their members and their territory.

The federal government recently reaffirmed its long-standing policy supporting self-determination by Indian tribes in a memorandum from the President on May 4, 1994. The memo stated:

> The United States Government has a unique legal relationship with Native American tribal governments as set forth in the Constitution of the United States, treaties, statutes, and court decisions. As executive departments and agencies undertake activities affecting Native American tribal rights or trust resources, such activities should be implemented in a knowledgeable, sensitive manner respectful of tribal sovereignty.[12]

Banks must recognize tribal sovereignty when doing business with an Indian tribe or its members because the Supreme Court has recognized that Indian tribes have authority to

---

[11] 25 USC § 4211(a). Effective October 1, 1996, the Native American Housing Assistance and Self-Determination Act of 1996 amended federal law to allow for a lease term, on tribal or individual trust land, not to exceed 50 years. Previously, tribes had 25-year leasing authority, which could be renewed, subject to BIA approval, for another 25 years. This provision may have discouraged some financial institutions from extending mortgage loans in Indian country, since many loans carry a 30-year term.

[12] President's memorandum of April 29, 1994, "Government-to-Government Relationships With Native American Tribal Governments," 59 Fed. Reg. 22,951 (1994).

license and regulate non-Indians engaging in commercial transactions with the tribe or its members.[13] Therefore, banks may be required to follow tribal law when conducting such commercial transactions.

In certain states, Congress has authorized the state courts to exercise civil jurisdiction over actions involving individual Indians in Indian country.[14] Public Law 280 may permit state courts to exercise jurisdiction in cases involving loans secured by the personal property of individual Indians.[15] However, because Public Law 280 did not provide the states with the authority to encumber property held in trust by the United States for Indians,[16] mortgages on individual Indian trust land may not be foreclosed in state court.[17]

What is sovereign immunity? Sovereign immunity is a governmental immunity that prevents a court from entering orders against the government in the absence of a clear waiver. As governments, Indian tribes enjoy sovereign immunity from suit under federal common law.[18] Tribal sovereign immunity is similar to the sovereign immunity of the United States or of individual states. Although tribal sovereign immunity does not cover individual Indians,[19] it does extend to tribal governmental agencies, such as Indian housing authorities.[20]

Which courts have civil jurisdiction in Indian country? Except as otherwise provided by federal law, tribal courts have exclusive civil jurisdiction over a suit by any person against an Indian for a claim arising in Indian country. Banks that wish to develop a mortgage lending program in Indian country should consult with local counsel familiar with Indian law in order to understand the implications of sovereign immunity and tribal court

---

[13] Merrion v. Jicarilla Apache Tribe, 455 U.S. 130, 144 (1982); Montana v. United States, 450 U.S. 544, 565 (1981).

[14] Act of Aug. 15, 1993, Pub. L. No. 280, 67 Stat. 588 (codified as amended at 18 USC § 1162, 25 USC §§ 1321-1326, and 28 USC § 1360) ("Public Law 280").

[15] It should be noted that Public Law 280 applies only to individual Indians and does not give state courts any jurisdiction over Indian tribes.

[16] 28 USC § 1360(b). The federal government has exclusive and protective jurisdiction over Indian trust land and Indian allotments, and federal approval is required for any alienation of Indian property.

[17] Boisclair v. Superior Court, 801 P.2d 305 (Cal. 1990).

[18] Santa Clara Pueblo v. Martinez, 436 U.S. 49, 58 (1978).

[19] Puyallup Tribe, Inc. v. Washington Game Dept., 433 U.S. 165 (1977).

[20] Weeks Construction, Inc. v. Oglala Sioux Housing Authority, 797 F.2d 668 (8th Cir. 1986).

jurisdiction over civil claims.

Despite tribal courts' exclusive jurisdiction over civil claims, some tribal governments have not yet adopted laws governing mortgage lending and foreclosure. In dealing with these governments, a bank may wish to help the tribe, the tribal court, and the tribe's counsel to enact laws facilitating private mortgage lending on the reservation.

The National Indian Justice Center and the Department of Housing and Urban Development's (HUD) Office of Native American Programs (ONAP) have published a comprehensive Tribal Housing Code,[21] including foreclosure procedures, required by the Section 184 Loan Guarantee Program. (See part III of this guide for further discussion of this program.) The code serves as a model to address issues that commonly arise in lending to Native Americans and to help tribal leaders make the choices needed to create the legal infrastructure necessary for private financing in Indian country.

What does the Native American Housing Assistance and Self-Determination Act of 1996 mean for financial institutions? The Native American Housing Assistance and Self-Determination Act of 1996[22] (NAHASDA) will likely change the landscape of affordable housing in Indian country. Rather than receiving public housing assistance in a piecemeal fashion under a number of programs, Indian tribes will receive a single, needs-based block grant.

The NAHASDA, which becomes effective October 1, 1997, separates Indian housing assistance from public housing assistance. One of its major objectives is to promote the development of private capital markets in Indian country and to allow such markets to operate and grow.[23]

The Secretary of HUD, through ONAP, will implement NAHASDA. Each fiscal year, the HUD Secretary will make block grants to Indian tribes that have submitted Indian housing plans that comply with the requirements of the program. With the block grant funds, recipient tribes will have the flexibility to design new programs, continue existing programs, and leverage additional housing resources through public-private partnerships with private lenders.

---

[21] Resource Directory, 1 Indian Hous. L.Q. 44 (1996). The Tribal Housing Code is published as part of the "Our Home" series under the title "Providing the Legal Infrastructure Necessary for Private Financing." To obtain copies, contact your local ONAP office, listed in appendix C of this guide.

[22] Pub. L. No. 104-330, 110 Stat. 4016 (codified at 25 U.S.C. § 4101 et seq. and in scattered sections of 42 U.S.C.).

[23] 25 USC § 4131(a)(5).

The block grants may be used for eligible affordable housing activities, which include:

- Indian housing assistance (modernization or operating assistance for housing previously developed or operated pursuant to a contract between HUD and an Indian housing authority);

- Acquisition, new construction, reconstruction, or moderate or substantial rehabilitation of affordable housing;

- Housing-related services for affordable housing, such as housing counseling, establishment of resident organizations, or energy auditing;

- Management services for affordable housing, including loan processing, inspections, and management of affordable housing projects;

- Safety, security, and law enforcement measures and activities appropriate to protect residents of affordable housing from crime; and

- Housing activities under model programs designed to carry out the purposes of the act and specifically approved by HUD.[24]

HUD recently issued proposed rules to implement NAHASDA.[25] The act provides that final regulations must be issued by HUD not later than September 1, 1997, to become effective October 1, 1997.[26]

---

[24] 25 USC § 4132.

[25] See 62 Fed. Reg. 35,718 (July 2, 1997) (proposing rules to be codified at 24 CFR parts 950, 953, 955, 1000, 1003, and 1005).

[26] 25 USC § 4116(b)(1).

Part II — Residential Mortgage Lending Process

Making mortgage loans in Indian country is like making mortgage loans anywhere else, with a few exceptions. This section provides a guide to those exceptions. (Because banks often use government-guaranteed programs to lend in Indian country, they will need to understand the specific requirements of the loan program. General information about some of these programs is included in part III of this guide.)

The Lending Process

Mortgage production usually proceeds in four phases: origination, processing, underwriting, and closing. Before the application process begins, a bank should consider whether a consumer needs pre-purchase counseling.

Pre-purchase counseling. Many Native American mortgage loan applicants living on a reservation are first-time home buyers who may not be familiar with the mortgage lending process in general, the requirements of a specific lender, or the various types of loans or loan guarantee programs available. According to many financial institutions, customer education is a key to lending successfully in Indian country.

To facilitate the homebuying process, a bank may sometimes recommend that the applicant obtain homeownership counseling. A bank that does not counsel applicants in-house may arrange with qualified third parties to supply such training.

Some of the topics that may be addressed in a pre-purchase homeownership counseling program include:

- What information a lender considers when an applicant applies for a mortgage loan;

- How an applicant can determine whether he or she is likely to qualify for financing;

- What financing options are available and which option(s) would be most suitable for the applicant;

- What barriers might exist that could prevent the applicant from qualifying, how to overcome the barriers, and whether there may be nontraditional financing programs for which the applicant may qualify;

- How to select a home that is suitable for the applicant's needs and financial means;

- How the homebuying process works, from identifying a property through closing; and

- How to be a responsible homeowner, in terms of both financial responsibility and home maintenance.

A list of housing counseling agencies approved by HUD may be found on the internet at http://www.aspensys.com/hcc/. Alternatively, banks can contact the Housing Counseling Clearinghouse at P.O. Box 9057, Gaithersburg, MD 20898-9998 or (800) 217-6970.

In addition, a bank may want to establish a partnership with a community organization or financial intermediary that assists both banks and prospective borrowers in the mortgage loan application process. To locate such an organization in its community, a bank may contact the OCC's community reinvestment development specialists, listed in appendix A, or the Community Development Division at (202) 874-4930.

Origination. For the purpose of this guide, origination consists of lending officers taking applications from prospective borrowers at the bank, on the Indian Reservation, or at any location convenient to the borrower and bank. Some banks reach out to customers on reservations by using mobile branches, mini-branches in supermarkets, or temporary booths at community events or festivals.

Usually, lending officers meet with prospective borrowers and take applications from them directly. Alternative origination methods may prove useful to banks extending mortgage loans in remote areas of Indian country. In addition to originating loans through face-to-face customer contacts in the bank, some banks originate loans by accepting applications submitted through home personal computers or through loan officers who take applications from borrowers in nonbank locations.

Processing. Processors verify information supplied by an applicant, order an appraisal, determine title status and whether title insurance is required, and, in Indian country, obtain BIA approval of the loan.

Appraisals. The requirements for obtaining an appraisal or evaluation when using the underlying real property as collateral are the same in Indian country as anywhere else. During the BIA approval process, described below, a BIA appraiser will review a commercially prepared appraisal or may choose to prepare his or her own.

Title status. A bank must determine the real property's title status when making a mortgage loan to be secured by an ownership interest in land or a lease. However, when title to the land is restricted or held in trust, the bank usually cannot go to a county records office to determine ownership.[27]

The BIA maintains title records on all real property held in trust or restricted status for a tribe or an individual Indian, whether such property is inside or outside the boundaries of an Indian reservation.[28] Once a bank receives an application for a mortgage loan secured by either an ownership or leasehold interest in Indian land, the bank should contact the BIA area office that has jurisdiction over the subject property. In some cases, it may also be necessary to contact the local BIA agency office or the tribe itself.[29]

The bank should provide the BIA with a letter requesting a title status report (TSR).[30] The letter must include the legal description of the real property and should include, if available, the allotment and tract number of the property and, if applicable, a plat or subdivision map number. Although the TSR and documents referred to in the TSR may be certified by the United States government, a TSR does not constitute a final title opinion or abstract of title providing recourse against the United States in case of errors or omissions. In order to protect its security interest, a bank may want to obtain an abstract of title or title insurance, as discussed below.

The bank's title search request will be sent to one of the BIA Land Title and Records Offices. The regional BIA Land Title and Records Offices are located in Anchorage, Alaska; Sacramento, California; Billings, Montana; Albuquerque, New Mexico; Muskogee/Anadarko, Oklahoma; Portland, Oregon; Aberdeen, South Dakota; and Arlington, Virginia. Each of these offices prepares TSRs for properties within their jurisdictions based on the ownership and encumbrance records of the BIA.

Banks often encounter delays in obtaining BIA title reports. Therefore, a bank should request the title report as soon as an application for a mortgage loan is made. The cost of a report depends on the amount of research required and the number of owners of the property.

Title insurance. Only a few firms offer title insurance for mortgage loans secured by an

---

[27] Oklahoma presents an exception to that rule. In Oklahoma, some title records for trust or restricted lands are maintained by the state or county recording system. For help in determining the appropriate location to conduct a title search, banks making mortgages in Oklahoma should consult their BIA area or agency office.

[28] See 25 CFR part 150 — Land Records and Title Documents.

[29] The BIA has 12 area offices across the country with 86 agency offices reporting to them. A list of the area offices is included in this guide as appendix B.

[30] A TSR is a detailed title report that, among other things, will reveal information about the owners of a property (who they are, their fractional interests, and how their interests were acquired) and the status of the property (whether it is held in trust or in restricted status and whether there are any encumbrances against it).

interest in Indian land. However, several title insurance companies are developing title insurance policies and underwriting standards for such loans. Fannie Mae has worked with title insurance companies to help them develop local programs. To obtain information about these companies, banks may contact Fannie Mae at (202) 752-7407.

BIA approval process. If a mortgage loan to an Indian is secured by interests in trust or restricted Indian land, it must be approved by the BIA.[31] BIA approval is not necessary for mortgages secured by fee simple land, even if it is located on a reservation, unless the fee simple land is owned by a tribe.

The BIA is streamlining and standardizing this approval process, which currently varies by region. The BIA area offices can answer questions about how the approval process works in their areas, specifically whether a bank should initiate the approval process with the area or agency office and whether the tribe maintains its own realty files.

Generally, the bank must submit the mortgage loan documents to the BIA area director or agency superintendent with jurisdiction over the property. Items the area director or agency superintendent may require include the following: mortgage or deed of trust; promissory note and security agreement; appraisal; evidence of title (TSR or abstract of title); and the borrower's loan application, credit report, and income verification. If the applicant is a self-employed businessperson, the area director or agency superintendent may also request the company's financial statements and business plan.

To approve the mortgage, the area director or agency superintendent must be reasonably certain that the applicant has the repayment capacity to avoid default and foreclosure. The BIA may also appraise the subject property to ensure that the borrower is not over-collateralizing the loan.

BIA approval benefits the bank by removing restrictions against encumbrances that otherwise apply to property held in trust or restricted status for an individual.[32] As a result, the bank will have authority to foreclose and take possession of the property interest upon the default of the borrower. The property interest in individual trust or restricted land could be the land itself or a leasehold. If it is tribal land, the property interest will be a leasehold, not the land itself. Failure by the bank to obtain BIA approval of the loan contract renders it void.

Underwriting. Underwriting involves evaluating whether the prospective borrower qualifies for the requested mortgage. Underwriters employ the bank's guidelines or those

---

[31] 25 CFR §§ 152.34 and 162.12.

[32] 25 USC § 483a and 25 CFR § 152.34.

of the mortgage program in which the bank participates, e.g., one extending a federal government guarantee.

Underwriters generally analyze loan applications by reviewing what are traditionally called the "four C's of credit." They are: the borrower's credit history, character (job stability and reliability), capacity to repay a loan, and collateral (condition and value of property). Collateral is the area that presents the most complexities for lenders extending mortgage loans in Indian country.

The ability to use Indian trust land as collateral depends on whether the land is held in trust for the tribe or the individual, as described in part I of this guide. Although holders of individual trust land or individual restricted fee land can mortgage their land directly or use a leasehold interest as collateral, neither tribal trust land nor tribal restricted fee land can be mortgaged directly. The tribe must issue a leasehold interest to the borrower, who uses that interest as collateral. Fee simple land held by an individual on an Indian reservation can be mortgaged in the same manner as privately owned land outside of the reservation.

In addition to taking interests in land to secure mortgage loans, national banks may secure a loan with other property interests, such as proceeds from land leases or natural resources, or interest income from trust funds held in tribal accounts by the BIA. Whether the collateral interest is in land or other property, underwriting standards should emphasize the borrower's ability to repay the loan from cash flow or net income rather than the sale of collateral. When the bank offers a low introductory interest rate, prudent underwriting analyzes repayment capacity at the end of the introductory rate term.

To increase efficiency, reduce costs, and expedite application decisions, many banks are using credit scoring tools for electronic evaluation of loan applicants. Such banks should recognize these tools' limitations, i.e., they may be unable to assess the creditworthiness of applicants who do not fit typical profiles — such as first-time homebuyers on Indian reservations.

Second review programs. Many banks are implementing second review procedures to assure themselves and the mortgage loan applicants that every effort has been made to qualify each applicant. Such programs, which may be very useful in Indian country, examine for a second time the characteristics and circumstances of applicants recommended for denial after an initial review. Internal or external panels can help the bank seek ways of approving these loans. Banks usually establish strict criteria for applicants afforded a second review.

Closing. After a loan is approved, the final phase is to close the loan, i.e., to disburse loan proceeds and to receive executed loan documents evidencing the borrower's debt and the bank's security interest in collateral.

Recording the lien. When a bank makes a loan secured by an interest in Indian land, the bank will require the borrower to execute a deed of trust, a mortgage, or other similar lien document. According to the BIA, once it approves these documents in the process described above, the bank has a valid lien. To further protect its interest, a bank should record the lien document along with the note with the county records office, tribal realty office, the BIA Land Title and Records Office, and the BIA agency office having jurisdiction over the land.

Portfolio Management

When the production phase is over, the bank should monitor and service its Indian mortgage portfolio in the same manner it manages its other real estate portfolios. Monitoring minimizes the effect that underperforming or defaulted loans could have on the bank's profitability. Programs that review the borrower's financial condition annually (or at other regular intervals) will help to spot potential repayment problems before a crisis occurs.

Effective loan monitoring to minimize delinquencies is particularly important when lending in Indian country. Government guarantee programs, which are often used in this market, may have more liberal lending standards than conventional programs. For example, some permit higher loan-to-value ratios, higher debt-to-income ratios, or lower requirements for savings on hand. To minimize delinquencies and foreclosures, some banks have adopted "enhanced" or "accelerated" servicing programs in which they closely monitor loans meeting relaxed credit criteria. If such loans become delinquent, the bank can immediately start working with the borrower.[33]

Homeowner's counseling for delinquent or defaulting borrowers. If a borrower is slow in making payments or has missed a payment, the bank may consider providing credit counseling to the borrower. The counseling program should describe the options, programs, and actions available to the borrower for resolving the delinquency or default. The bank may provide this counseling itself or direct the borrower to a third party. Typically, the same agencies that counsel first-time homebuyers provide credit counseling.

Foreclosure

Because Indian tribes are sovereign nations and typically have jurisdiction over mortgage transactions, lenders must resolve most foreclosures in tribal courts.

---

[33] See also OCC Advisory Letter 97-3, issued March 7, 1997, on effective credit underwriting standards and portfolio credit risk management; and OCC Advisory Letter 97-7, issued July 23, 1997, on affordable mortgage portfolios.

As discussed earlier, some tribal governments have adopted procedures to allow foreclosure actions to be pursued in tribal courts. Many tribal codes prescribe how creditors can repossess collateral or otherwise obtain remedies in the event of default.

The extent to which specific remedies are available to creditors depends on whether the tribal government has adopted procedures. In some cases, tribal governments may be willing to enact new ordinances or resolutions in order to ensure that the desired remedies are, in fact, available.

Assuming that a bank has obtained BIA approval of its mortgage, it may bring a foreclosure action to levy upon the interest (either the land itself or a leasehold interest) securing the loan. Tribal law governs the foreclosure process. Lenders that have been authorized by a tribal court to levy upon the secured interest may seek guidance from BIA area directors.

Part III — Types of Mortgage Loan Programs

Banks can provide mortgage loans in Indian country that meet their conventional mortgage lending guidelines and underwriting criteria. They can also participate in special mortgage programs that make mortgage money available to Native Americans. Some of these programs are summarized below. Information about whom to contact for additional information is listed in the discussion of each program.

Direct Mortgage Programs

Department of Housing and Urban Development

- Office of Native American Programs -- Section 184

What does the program cover? Under the provisions of section 184 of the Housing and Community Development Act of 1992, Congress created the Section 184 Loan Guarantee Program to increase the availability of mortgage capital in Indian country. The program covers single-family residential loans made by eligible lenders to eligible Native Americans whose home sites are on Indian land. Commercial structures are not eligible for the Section 184 program. The guarantee covers 100 percent of the outstanding principal and interest as well as other necessary and allowable expenses. Borrowers make a modest down payment and pay a fee of 1 percent for the guarantee. The required terms and uses of the loan are flexible so that they may be tailored to the needs of the individual borrower.

How are banks involved? Banks automatically qualify as a lender under the Section 184 program if they are approved for participation in the Federal Housing Administration's (FHA) single-family mortgage insurance program. Lenders who are not FHA-approved may qualify for the Section 184 program by demonstrating to HUD that the U.S. Department of Veterans Affairs or U.S. Department of Agriculture has authorized them as lenders, or that they are supervised, approved, regulated, or insured by any agency of the federal government.

Lenders accept and process borrowers' applications for financing, and, if the borrower qualifies, submit the loan application package to HUD requesting a firm commitment under Section 184. Once HUD approves the firm commitment and a closing takes place, the lender makes the loan to the borrower. The loan may be held in portfolio or sold. In the event of default, the lender has the option of either foreclosing or requesting assignment of the loan to HUD.

Who can use the program? Eligible borrowers include:

- An Indian family or individual who will occupy the property as a principal residence and who has met the credit and underwriting standards specified by the program.

- An Indian Housing Authority (IHA) or Tribally Designated Housing Entity (TDHE) that may borrow funds to create IHA- or TDHE-owned rental housing or to develop single-family homes for sale to eligible borrowers.

- An Indian tribe that, like the IHAs or TDHEs, may borrow funds to create tribe-owned rental housing or to develop single-family homes for sale to eligible borrowers.

How is the program administered? ONAP administers the Section 184 program. Individuals, IHAs, TDHEs, and Indian tribes are responsible for submitting to private lenders an application containing information on the borrower's qualifications for mortgage financing.

Before a borrower can submit an application to a private lender, a tribe must enact policies and procedures for foreclosure and eviction actions in its tribal court system. In the alternative, the tribe could name a state or county court to assume jurisdiction and enforce state or county foreclosure procedures.

Tribes may coordinate the program by assisting borrowers with loan applications, leasing trust land for home sites, and providing financial assistance to borrowers.

How does one apply? Native American borrowers work directly with private lenders and their tribes to apply for a housing loan. Lenders then conduct the necessary loan underwriting analysis and coordinate with HUD regarding loan approval and commitment.

For more information about the HUD Section 184 program, banks or tribes may contact their local ONAP office, listed in appendix C.

Department of Veterans Affairs

- VA Direct Home Loans for Native American Veterans Living on Trust Lands

What does the program cover? A Department of Veterans Affairs (VA) direct loan can be used to purchase, construct, or improve a home on Native American trust land. VA direct loans are generally limited to the cost of the home or $80,000, whichever is less.

How are banks involved? Because the VA makes these loans directly, banks' involvement is limited. However, in some parts of the country, VA has contracted with banks to package and process VA direct home loans. For this service, the banks are paid a fee.

Who can use the program? VA direct loans are available to all eligible Native American veterans who meet credit and income qualifications. Veterans who have been honorably discharged from active duty are eligible.

How is the program administered? The VA administers its direct home loan program. The initial appropriation for this pilot program will support a total of $58 million worth of loans. The authority to make direct loans under this pilot program expires October 1, 1997, unless the program is extended.

How does one apply? A Native American veteran must have a certificate of eligibility before he or she can apply for a VA direct home loan. A veteran who does not have a certificate can obtain one by applying to the local VA office on VA form 26-1880.

To apply for a loan, the veteran should contact either the local housing authority or the local VA regional office, listed in appendix D. The VA nationwide toll-free number is 1-800-827-1000.

- VA Loan Guarantee Program

Eligible veterans, including Native American veterans, may apply for loans guaranteed by the VA. The guarantee program is intended to encourage lenders to offer all veterans loans with more favorable terms. VA-guaranteed loans are made by private lenders such as banks, savings and loan associations, or mortgage companies. For more information about VA-guaranteed loans, banks can call 1-800-827-1000.

Department of Agriculture

- Rural Housing Service — Rural Housing Native American Pilot Loan Program

What does the program cover? The Rural Housing Native American Pilot (RHNAP) Loan Program was jointly developed by the Rural Housing Service (RHS) and Fannie Mae. In this program, the RHS guarantees loans made on tribal land. The pilot is modeled after the Section 502 Guaranteed Rural Housing (GRH) loan program, which was modified to work on trust lands. The loans are 30-year fixed rate loans and can be for the purchase of existing homes or for new construction. The loan can be for 100 percent of the value of the property.

Borrowers qualifying for RHNAP loans may use the funds to purchase single-family, owner-occupied, principal residences that qualify as "modest rural housing" (including units in condominiums, planned unit developments, and manufactured housing that is permanently affixed to the property). Homes must be located on tribal trust or restricted

21

fee simple lands owned by tribes. Individual allotments and unrestricted fee simple lands are not eligible.

How are banks involved? Lenders who have been approved by both RHS and Fannie Mae can originate RHSAP loans.

Who can use the program? Eligible borrowers include individual members of federally recognized tribes that have been approved by RHS to participate in the pilot program. There are currently 16 tribal governments that have been selected for the pilot. They are: Gila River and Navajo Nation in Arizona; San Juan Pueblo and Poaque Pueblo in New Mexico; Salish-Kootenai and Chippewa-Cree in Montana; Lac Courte Oreilles and Oneida in Wisconsin; Grand Traverse Band of Chippewa Indians and Sault Ste. Marie Tribe of Chippewa Indians in Michigan; Seminole in Florida; Cheyenne River Sioux in South Dakota; Omaha in Nebraska; Oneida in New York; Fort Mojave in Nevada; and Pala Band of Mission Indians in California.

How does one apply? An eligible borrower applies directly to an RHS/Fannie Mae-approved lender.

For more information about the RHNAP loan program, banks can contact the Rural Housing Services state offices, listed in appendix E.

Federal Home Loan Bank System

The Federal Home Loan Bank (FHLB) System is a privately capitalized, cooperative, government-sponsored enterprise created by Congress in 1932. Consisting of twelve regional FHLBs, the system's mission is to support the residential mortgage lending and community development lending of its member-stockholders. Eligible members include commercial banks, savings institutions, credit unions, and insurance companies.

The FHLB System provides economical wholesale credit and technical assistance to its members. Its member-stockholders receive an attractive and safe investment. An institution may apply for membership by contacting the FHLB in its area. A list of the FHLBs is included in appendix F.

The FHLB System's homebuyer assistance programs are available through FHLB members to all eligible borrowers, including Native Americans. The FHLB of Des Moines' Model American Indian Partnership Project increased a tribal entity's funding options by making it an FHLB nonmember borrower. For more information about this pilot program, contact the FHLB of Des Moines.

- FHLB Affordable Housing Program

What does the program cover? Under the Affordable Housing Program (AHP), the FHLBs subsidize long-term housing finance for very low-, low-, and moderate-income families through direct subsidies (grants) or subsidized advances (loans) to financial institution lenders that are stockholders in the FHLB System. These grants or loans are used to buy, build, or rehabilitate owner-occupied or affordable rental housing.

The FHLBs contribute the greater of $100 million or 10 percent of the system's net income each year to the AHP. In 1997, the FHLB System expects to provide approximately $119.7 million in AHP funds.

How are banks involved? Nonprofit sponsors, such as community development corporations, must apply for these direct subsidies and subsidized advances through FHLB member-stockholders.

Who can use the program? Nonprofit organizations, for-profit developers, and state and local agencies are eligible to apply through FHLB member-stockholders.

How is the program administered? The funds are distributed by district through a semiannual competitive grant. All FHLB member-stockholders may compete for these funds through their FHLB.

How does a borrower apply? Individual borrowers receive their funds through nonprofit organizations, for-profit developers, and state and local agencies, which must apply for these AHP funds through FHLB member-stockholders.

—   AHP Homeowner Set-Aside

What does the program cover? Households may receive up to $10,000 for down payment, closing, and counseling costs on the purchase or rehabilitation of owner-occupied property. If a homeowner sells the home within five years of receiving the AHP funds, the homeowner must repay a portion of the funds reduced pro-rata for each year of ownership of the home.

Who can use the program? Participating households must have incomes of no more than 80 percent of area median income and must complete a homebuyer or homeowner counseling program.

How is the program administered? Each FHLB sets aside $1.5 million or 15 percent of their annual required AHP contribution, whichever is greater, for one or more homeownership set-aside programs. If demand for funds exceeds the supply, the FHLB may use up to $1.5 million or 15 percent of its annual required AHP contribution for the subsequent year.

How does one apply? Borrowers submit applications through FHLB member-stockholders.

- FHLB Community Investment Program

What does the program cover? The Community Investment Program (CIP) provides favorably priced funding to member-stockholders for affordable housing, economic development, and commercial revitalization in the markets the FHLBs serve.

Funds may be used for home mortgages and improvements; rental housing; modified housing for the handicapped; capital improvement for small business; construction; historic preservation; development of industrial facilities, civic centers, and social service facilities; and community health care facilities. CIP housing finance funds must benefit families or individuals with incomes of no more than 115 percent of the area median. CIP funds may also be used for commercial and economic development projects that benefit low- and moderate-income households (with incomes up to 80 percent of the median for the area) or that are located in low- and moderate-income neighborhoods.

How are banks involved? FHLB member-stockholders may apply for CIP funds.

Who can use the program? Institutions holding stock in the FHLB System.

How is the program administered? CIP is a noncompetitive advance program. The advances are made at the district level within the FHLB system. Stockholder financial institutions apply for CIP funds through the FHLB in which they are stockholders.

How does a borrower apply? All applications must be submitted through FHLB stockholders. All families or individuals with incomes of 80 percent of the area median or less, including Native American families and individuals, may potentially benefit from CIP funds.

For more information on any of these programs, banks should contact their local FHLB.

Secondary Market

To help increase mortgage lending in Indian country, banks may obtain capital by packaging mortgage loans made in programs especially for Native Americans and selling them on the secondary market. Fannie Mae and Freddie Mac (Federal Home Loan Mortgage Corporation) are government-sponsored enterprises that buy mortgage loans made to Native Americans.

Fannie Mae

Fannie Mae is a federally chartered private corporation with the public mission of promoting housing for all Americans by attracting investment capital into mortgage lending. Fannie Mae has been actively working with a variety of partners, the BIA, and a number of Indian tribes to increase mortgage financing opportunities for Native Americans.

What loans will Fannie Mae buy? Fannie Mae will buy the following loans:

- Permanent loans guaranteed by HUD under the Native American Housing Loan Guarantee Program (Section 184).

- Section 184 construction/permanent loans. (There is a single closing for the construction/permanent mortgage loan, with a single interest rate.)

- Loans made under the Native American FHA Mortgage Insurance Program (HUD 248), including both permanent and construction/permanent loans. These loans are insured by the FHA under section 248 of the National Housing Act.

- Section 502 Guaranteed RHS loans under the Rural Housing Native American Pilot. These loans will be available for selected tribes working in partnership with Fannie Mae and RHS.

- Conventional loans for Native Americans living on trust or restricted lands under a Fannie Mae Native American Conventional Lending Initiative. A tribe's separate approval is required for participation.

What lenders may sell loans to Fannie Mae? A lender must be approved as a Fannie Mae seller/servicer in order to sell loans to Fannie Mae. To obtain approval or more information about Fannie Mae's Native American loan purchase programs, lenders should contact their Fannie Mae lead regional office. Fannie Mae regional offices are listed in appendix G.

Freddie Mac

Freddie Mac is a federally chartered private corporation established by Congress in 1970 to create a continuous flow of funds to mortgage lenders in support of homeownership and rental housing. Freddie Mac is also working to increase lending to Native Americans in Indian country.

What loans will Freddie Mac buy? On a negotiated basis, Freddie Mac will purchase the following eligible mortgage loans:

- Fifteen-, twenty-, and thirty-year mortgage loans made under the HUD Section 184

Indian Housing Loan Guarantee Program for one- to four-unit dwellings located on both fee simple and restricted lands.

- Fifteen-, twenty-, and thirty-year mortgage loans originated for Native American, Indian tribe, Alaskan Native, and New Mexican Pueblo homebuyers under the FHA Section 248 Native American Mortgages Program. These mortgage loans may only be made on properties located on Indian reservations and other restricted lands, not on lands owned in fee simple.

What lenders may sell loans to Freddie Mac? Any lender approved by Freddie Mac. Banks wishing to request an eligibility package may call 1-800-FREDDIE (373-3343) or contact the main office at 8200 Jones Branch Drive, McLean, Virginia 22102.

Part IV — Compliance Issues

Banks must comply with all consumer protection statutes applicable to residential lending when they make home loans secured by interests in Indian land. The OCC's Comptroller's Handbook booklets on consumer compliance examination provide more detailed information about consumer protection laws.

The fair lending statutes, the Equal Credit Opportunity Act[34] (ECOA) and the Fair Housing Act[35] (FH Act), apply to banks that make home loans in Indian country just as they apply to banks that make home loans elsewhere. Because banks frequently ask questions regarding potential lending discrimination in Indian country, a discussion of lending discrimination follows. Interested parties may also refer to the section in the Comptroller's Handbook on fair lending for more detailed information about compliance with fair lending laws.[36]

Fair Lending Statutes

The ECOA prohibits discrimination in any part of a credit transaction and applies to any extension of credit, including extensions of credit to small businesses, corporations, partnerships, and trusts. It prohibits discrimination based on race, color, or national origin, among other factors.

The FH Act prohibits discrimination in all parts of residential real-estate related transactions. The FH Act also prohibits discrimination based on race, color, or national origin, among other factors.

Discriminating in a credit transaction against persons because they are Native Americans violates the ECOA and, if the transaction is related to residential real estate, it violates the FH Act.

Types of lending discrimination. The courts have recognized three methods of proof of lending discrimination under the ECOA and the FH Act: overt evidence of discrimination, evidence of disparate treatment, and evidence of disparate impact.

Overt evidence of discrimination. Overt evidence of discrimination occurs when a lender openly discriminates in a prohibited manner, even if a lender expresses — but does not act on — a discriminatory preference. For example, a lending officer says to a customer, "We

---

[34] 15 USC § 1691 et seq.

[35] 42 USC § 3601 et seq.

[36] See also Policy Statement on Discrimination in Lending, 59 Fed. Reg. 18,266 (1994).

do not like to make home mortgage loans to Native Americans, but the law says we cannot discriminate, and we have to comply with the law." This statement violates the FH Act's prohibition on statements expressing a discriminatory preference and may discourage, in violation of ECOA, an applicant, on a prohibited basis, from applying for a loan.

Evidence of disparate treatment. Disparate treatment occurs when a lender treats a credit applicant differently in a prohibited way. Evidence of disparate treatment does not require showing that the treatment was motivated by prejudice or a conscious intention to discriminate against a person.

If a lender appears to have treated similar applicants differently on the basis of a prohibited factor, it must explain the apparent difference. If the lender is unable to provide a credible and legitimate nondiscriminatory explanation for the difference in treatment, a court will likely conclude that the difference is due to discrimination.

Reliance on generalizations about lending to Native Americans on reservations, even if the generalizations are based on group statistics, can amount to disparate treatment. For example, although the rate of default may be higher on loans made to Native Americans on a reservation, a court could find disparate treatment if a bank treated a particular Native American applicant differently as a result of this generalization. A bank must consider the creditworthiness of each individual applicant.

Another example of how disparate treatment might occur is "redlining," whereby lenders refuse to make residential loans to borrowers or impose more onerous terms on them because of the predominant race, national origin, etc., of the residents of the neighborhood in which the property is located. Redlining on a prohibited basis violates both the FH Act and the ECOA.

Evidence of disparate impact. When a lender applies a policy or practice that is neutral on its face equally to credit applicants, but the policy or practice has a disproportionate adverse impact on applicants of a particular racial/ethnic group, the policy or practice may have an illegal "disparate impact."

Although the precise contours of the law on disparate impact as it applies to lending discrimination are under development, it is well settled that proof of discrimination using a disparate impact analysis proceeds in several steps. The fact that a policy or practice has a disproportionate adverse impact on credit applicants of a particular racial/ethnic group does not by itself establish a violation. If the policy or practice is justified by "business necessity," the lender is not violating fair lending laws unless the same business purpose can be achieved by a policy or practice that does not have a disproportionate impact.

Some longstanding bank policies may affect Native American residents of an Indian reservation differently than they affect others. For example, a bank may, in part, judge an applicant's creditworthiness on "length of time employed." Native Americans may be more likely to be employed in a number of successive temporary jobs than is the rest of the local population. If the difference in adverse impact were significantly disproportionate, the bank would need to justify the use of "length of time employed" as a business necessity. Even if the bank could meet this test, it would still be violating ECOA and the FH Act if a less discriminatory alternative, e.g., continuity of income, whether or not from employment or the same job, could serve the same purpose with a less discriminatory effect.

Risk- and cost-based pricing. Banks sometimes assert that the risks or costs associated with making loans to people on a reservation are higher than those associated with loans to people located elsewhere. For example, the BIA approval process may increase the cost of making a mortgage. Banks, therefore, may assert a need to price loan products higher if the borrower resides on an Indian reservation.

Lenders may consider risk and cost in setting prices and other terms and conditions for loans. However, pricing policies should be based on legitimate risk and cost factors; they should not be hypothetical or speculative, or based on generalized assumptions. Pricing policies should be evaluated to ensure that pricing differences are supported by documented differences in risks and costs and are applied in a nondiscriminatory manner.

Community Reinvestment Act

Under the Community Reinvestment Act (CRA), financial institutions are encouraged to help meet the credit needs of their entire communities. The OCC takes into account a bank's record of helping to meet community credit needs when the bank files a corporate application with the OCC.

Although banks' lending and investments in Indian communities have always been considered in CRA evaluations, the new CRA regulations[37] issued in 1995 inform banks that lending to, investing in, and providing banking services to Indian country will receive favorable CRA consideration. The supplementary information provided with the rule encourages lending institutions to consult with tribal governments when appropriate.

Most importantly, the rule recognizes and rewards the efforts of lenders that use innovative or flexible underwriting methods, in a safe and sound manner, to address nettlesome credit availability problems such as those facing Native Americans living on trust lands. All in all, mortgage lending on an Indian reservation that is part of its community may be an important part of a bank's CRA performance record.

---

[37] Community Reinvestment Act Regulations, 60 Fed. Reg. 22,156 (May 4, 1995) (codified at 12 CFR part 25).

Appendixes

Appendix A
OCC Community Reinvestment and Development (CRDs) Specialists

The mission of the OCC's CRD program is to facilitate partnerships, provide technical assistance for banks and their community partners, and encourage investment, lending, and services to low- and moderate-income individuals and small businesses. The CRD specialists provide training and advice to national banks, communities, and bank examiners on best practices, options for satisfying CRA responsibilities, and how to expand access to credit and capital. They can also serve as a resource for national banks establishing contacts and programs with Indian tribes in their communities.

Northeastern District — Connecticut, Delaware, District of Columbia, Maine, Maryland, Massachusetts, New Hampshire, New Jersey, New York, Pennsylvania, Rhode Island, Puerto Rico, and the Virgin Islands.

Stephen Davey	(212) 790-4055	fax (212)790-4098
Denise Kirk-Murray	(212) 790-4055	fax (212)790-4098

Southeastern District — Alabama, Florida, Georgia, Mississippi, North Carolina, South Carolina, Tennessee, Virginia, and West Virginia.

Karol Klim	(404) 588-4515	fax (404) 588-4532
Nancy Gresham-Jones	(404) 588-4515	fax (404) 588-4532

Central District — Illinois, Indiana, Kentucky, Michigan, Ohio, and Wisconsin.

Roosevelt Washington	(312) 360-8884	fax (312) 435-0951
Paul Ginger	(312) 360-8876	fax (312) 435-0951

Midwestern District — Iowa, Kansas, Minnesota, Missouri, Nebraska, and the Dakotas.

Annette Lepique	(816) 556-1832	fax (816) 556-1892
Bradley Streeter	(816) 556-1836	fax (816) 556-1892

Southwestern District — Arkansas, Louisiana, New Mexico, Oklahoma, and Texas.

David Lewis	(214) 720-7027	fax (214) 720-7000
Don Smith	(214) 720-7028	fax (214) 720-7000

Western District — Alaska, Arizona, California, Colorado, Hawaii, Idaho, Montana, Nevada, Oregon, Utah, Washington, Wyoming, and Guam.

Anna Alvarez Boyd	(415) 545-5939	fax (415) 545-5925
Julia Brown	(415) 545-5956	fax (415) 545-5925

Appendix B
Bureau of Indian Affairs Area Offices

Aberdeen Area Office
Bureau of Indian Affairs
115 4th Avenue, SE
Aberdeen, SD 37401
(605) 226-7343 Fax (605)228-7448

Nebraska, North Dakota, and South Dakota

Albuquerque Area Office
Bureau of Indian Affairs
615 First Street, NW
P.O. Box 26567
Albuquerque, NM 87125
(505)766-3754 Fax (505)766-1964

Colorado and New Mexico

Anadarko Area Office
Bureau of Indian Affairs
WCD Office Complex
P.O. Box 368
Anadarko, OK 73005
(405) 247-6673 Fax (405)247-2242

Kansas and West Oklahoma

Billings Area Office
Bureau of Indian Affairs
316 North 26th Street
Billings, MT 59101
(406) 247-7943 Fax (406) 247-7976

Montana and Wyoming

Eastern Area Office
Bureau of Indian Affairs
3701 N. Fairfax Drive
Mail Stop 260-VASQ.
Arlington, VA 22203
(703) 235-2571 Fax (703) 235-8610

New York, Maine, Louisiana, Florida, North Carolina, and Mississippi

Juneau Area Office
Bureau of Indian Affairs
P.O. Box 255200
Juneau, AK 99802-5520
(907) 586-7177 Fax (907) 586-7169

Alaska

Minneapolis Area Office
Bureau of Indian Affairs
331 South Second Avenue
Minneapolis, MN 55401
(612) 373-1000 Fax (612) 373-1186

Minnesota, Iowa, Mich, and Wisconsin

Muskogee Area Office
Bureau of Indian Affairs
Old Federal Building
101 North 5th Street
Muskogee, OK 74401
(918) 687-2296 Fax (918) 687-2571

East Oklahoma

Appendix B — Bureau of Indian Affairs Area Offices (continued)

Navajo Area Office
Bureau of Indian Affairs
P.O. Box 1060
Gallup, NM 87305
(505) 863-8314 Fax (505) 863-8245

Navajo Reservation Only – Arizona, Utah, and
  New Mexico

Phoenix Area Office
Bureau of Indian Affairs
One North First Street
P.O. Box 10
Phoenix, AZ 85001
(602) 379-6600 Fax (602) 379-4413

Arizona, Nevada, Utah, California, and Idaho

Portland Area Office
Bureau of Indian Affairs
911 NE 11th Avenue
Portland, OR 97232
(503)231-6702 Fax (503) 231-2201

Oregon, Washington, and Idaho

Sacramento Area Office
Bureau of Indian Affairs
2800 Cottage Way
Sacramento, CA 95825
(916) 979-2600 Fax(916) 979-2569

California

Central Office
1849 C Street, NW
Washington, DC 20240
(202)208-3671

Appendix C
Department of Housing and Urban Development
Office of Native American Programs (ONAP) Regional Offices

East of the Mississippi River and Iowa

Eastern/Woodlands Office of Native American Programs
U.S. Department of Housing and Urban Development
77 West Jackson Boulevard, 24th Floor
Chicago, IL 60604-3507
(312) 886-4532

Louisiana, Missouri, Kansas, Oklahoma, and Texas

Southern Plains Office of Native American Programs
U.S. Department of Housing and Urban Development
500 West Main Street, Suite 400
Oklahoma City, OK 73012
(405) 553-7520
TDD Number: 405-231-4403

Colorado, Montana, Nebraska, North Dakota, South Dakota, and Wyoming

Northern Plains Office of Native American Programs
U.S. Department of Housing and Urban Development
First Interstate Tower North
633 17th Street
Denver, CO 80202-3607
(303) 672-5465
TDD Number: 303-844-6158

Arizona, California, New Mexico, Nevada

Southwest Office of Native American Programs
U.S. Department of Housing and Urban Development
Two Arizona Center
400 North Fifth Street, Suite 1650
Phoenix, AZ 85004-2361
(602) 379-4156
TDD Number: 602-379-4461

Idaho, Oregon, and Washington

Northwest Office of Native American Programs
U.S. Department of Housing and Urban Development
909 First Avenue, Suite 300
Seattle, WA 98104-1000
(206) 220-5270
TDD Number: (206) 220-5185

Alaska

Alaska Office of Native American Programs
U.S. Department of Housing and Urban Development
949 East 36th Avenue, Suite 401
Anchorage, AK 99508-4399
(907) 271-4633
TDD Number: (907) 271-4328

National Office of Native American Programs
1999 Broadway, Suite 3390, Box 90
Denver, Colorado 80127
(303) 675-1600 FAX (303) 675-1660
Internet address: Sec184_loans@hud.gov

Appendix D
Department of Veteran Affairs Regional Offices

Alabama
474 South Court Street
Montgomery, AL 36104
(205)223-7187

Alaska
2925 DeBarr Road
Anchorage, AK 99508
(907) 257-4736

Arizona
3225 North Central Avenue
Phoenix, AZ 85012
(602) 640-4758

Arkansas
P.O. Box 1280
Building 65, Fort Roots
North Little Rock, AR 72115
(501) 370-3760

California
Federal Building
11000 Wilshire Blvd
Los Angeles, CA 90024
(310) 575-7192

California
Oakland Federal Building
1301 Clay Street
Oakland, CA 94612-5209
(510) 637-1126

Colorado
P.O. Box 25126
44 Union Blvd
Denver, CO 80225
(303) 980-2860

Connecticut
VA Medical and Regional Office Center
450 Main Street
Hartford, CT 06103
(603) 666-7527

Delaware
VA Medical and Regional Office Center
1601 Kirkwood Highway
Wilmington, DE 19805
(215) 951-7847

District of Columbia
941 N.Capitol Street, NE
Washington, DC 20421
(202) 208-1318

Florida
P.O. Box 1437, 144 First Avenue, South
St. Petersburg, FL 33731
(813) 893-3812

Georgia
730 Peachtree Street, NE
Atlanta, GA 30365
(404) 347-3488

Hawaii
PJKK Federal Building
300 Ala Moana Blvd
Honolulu, HI 96813
(808) 541-1480

Idaho
Federal Buidling and U.S. Courthouse
550 West Fort Street, Box 044
Boise, ID 83724
(208) 334-1397

Ilinois
536 S. Clark Street, P.O. Box 8136
Chicago, IL 60680
(312) 353-4065

Indiana
575 N. Pennsylvania Street
Indianapolis, IN 46204
(317) 226-7810

Iowa
210 Walnut Street
Des Moines, IA 50309
(515) 284-4829

Kansas
VA Medical and Regional Office Center
5500 E. Kellogg
Wichita, KS 67218
(316) 688-6720

Appendix D — Department of Veterans Affairs Regional Offices (continued)

Kentucky
545 South 3rd Street
Louisville, KY 40202
(502) 582-6025

Louisiana
701 Loyola Avenue
New Orleans, LA 70113
(504) 589-6412

Maine
VA Medical and Regional Office
Route 17 East
Togus, ME 04330
(603) 666-7527

Maryland [1]
Center Federal Building
31 Hopkins Plaza
Baltimore, MD 21201
(410) 962-4250

Massachusetts
J.F.K. Federal Building
Boston, MA 02203
(603) 666-7527

Michigan
477 Michigan Avenue
Detroit, MI 48226
(313) 226-4224

Minnesota
VA Regional Office and Insurance Center
One Federal Drive, Fort Snelling
St. Paul, MN 55111
(612) 725-3064

Mississippi
100 W. Capitol Street
Jackson, MS 39269
(601) 965-4825

Missouri
1520 Market Street
St. Louis, MO 63103
(314) 539-3147

Montana
VA Medical and Regional Office Center
Fort Harrison, MT 59636
(406) 447-7901

Nebraska
5631 South 48th Street
Lincoln, NE 68516
(402) 437-5032

Nevada [2]
1201 Terminal Way
Reno, NV 89520
(415) 744-7495

New Hampshire
275 Chestnut Street
Manchester, NH 03101
(603) 666-7527

New Jersey
20 Washington Place
Newark, NJ 07102
(201) 645-3470

New Mexico
500 Gold Avenue, SW
Albuquerque, NM 87102
(505) 766-2209

New York
Federal Building
111 West Huron Street
Buffalo, NY 14202
(716) 846-5291

New York
252 Seventh Avenue at
 24th Street
New York, NY 10001
(212) 620-6421

North Carolina
251 North Main Street
Winston-Salem, NC 27155
(919) 631-5447

North Dakota
VA Medical and Regional Office Center
2101 Elm Street
Fargo, ND 58102-2498
(612) 725-3064

Ohio
1240 East Ninth Street
Cleveland, OH 44199
(216) 522-3614

Appendix D — Department of Veterans Affairs Regional Offices (continued)

Oklahoma
125 South Main Street
Muskogee, OK 74401
(918) 687-2158

Oregon
Federal Building
1220 Southwest Third Avenue
Portland, OR 97204
(503) 326-2475

Pennsylvania
P.O. Box 8079
5000 Wissahickon Avenue
Philadelphia, PA 19101
(215) 951-7847

Pennsylvania
1000 Liberty Avenue
Pittsburgh, PA 15222
(412) 644-6660

Puerto Rico
GPO Box 4867
San Juan, PR 00936
(809) 766-5120

Rhode Island
380 Westminster Mall
Providence, RI 02903
(603) 666-7527

South Carolina
1801 Assembly Street
Columbia, SC 29201
(803) 765-5616

South Dakota
VA Medical and Regional Office Center
P.O. Box 5046, 2501 West 22nd Street
Sioux Falls, SD 57117
(612) 725-3064

Tennessee
110 9th Avenue, South 8900
Nashville, TN 37203
(615) 736-5243

Texas
Lakes at 610 Drive
Houston, TX 77054
(713) 660-4134

Texas
1400 North Valley Mills Drive
Waco, TX 76799
(817) 757-6822

Utah
P.O. Box 11500
125 South State Street
Salt Lake City, UT 84147
(801) 524-3411

Vermont
VA Medical and Regional Office Center
White River Junction, VT 05001
(603) 666-7527

Virginia [3]
210 Franklin Road, SW
Roanoke, VA 24011
(703) 982-4736

Washington [4]
Federal Building
915 Second Avenue
Seattle, WA 98174
(206) 220-6126

West Virginia [5]
640 4th Avenue
Huntington, WV 25701
(304) 529-5414

Wisconsin
Building 6
5000 West National Avenue
Milwaukee, WI 53295
(414) 382-5050

Wyoming
VA Medical and Regional Office Center
2360 Eash Pershing Blvd
Cheyenne, WY 82001
(303) 980-2860

Appendix D — Department of Veterans Affairs Regional Offices (continued)

Notes: (1) Montgomery and Prince Georges counties in Maryland are handled by Washington, D.C.
(2) Clark and Lincoln counties, Nevada, are handled in Los Angeles, California.
(3) Arlington, Farifax, Loudoun, Prince William, Spotsylvania and Stafford counties and the cities of Alexandria, Fairfax, Falls Church, and Fredericksburg in Virginia are handled by Washington, D.C.
(4) Clark, Klickitat, and Skamania counties in the state of Washington are handled by Portland, Oregon.
(5) Brooke, Hancock, Marshall, and Ohio counties in West Virginia are handled by Pittsburgh, Pennsylvania.

Appendix E
Rural Housing Service (RHS)

Guaranteed Rural Housing (GRH) Program's State Office Contacts

Alabama	Louis Rambo	(334) 279-3440
Alaska	Karen LaMouria	(907) 745-2176
Arizona	Steve Kimmel	(602) 280-8762
Arkansas	Ronnie Moore	(501) 324-6273
California	Logan Wilson	(916) 668-2094
Colorado	Donald Pierce	(303) 236-2801 ext 114
Delaware, Maryland	Gerald Chandler	(302) 697-4314
Florida	Bob Coordsen	(352) 338-3435
Georgia	Douglas Canup	(706) 546-2169
Hawaii	Mark Huggins	(808) 933-3007
Idaho	Ronnie Atkins	(208) 378-5627
Illinois	Cathy McNeal	(217) 398-5412 ext 259
Indiana	Vince Maloney	(317) 290-3115
Iowa	Robyn Holdorf	(515) 284-4486
Kansas	Martin Fee	(913) 271-2720
Kentucky	Don Johnson	(606) 224-7322
Louisiana	Debbie Redfearn	(318) 473-7630
Maine	Jim Berry	(207) 324-7012
Massachusetts, Connecticut, Rhode Island	Donald Colburn	(413) 253-4326
Michigan	Ernie Schuette	(517) 337-6635
Minnesota	Renee Woodard	(612) 290-3911
Mississippi	Ken Wright	(601) 965-4325
Missouri	Randall Griffith	(314) 876-0990
Montana	Mary Lou Falconer	(406) 585-2515
Nebraska	Michael Buethe	(402) 437-5557
Nevada	Clayre Moiola	(702) 738-8468
New Jersey	Neal Hayes	(609) 265-3633
New Mexico	Eric Schmieder	(505) 761-4944
New York	Peter Lorey	(315) 477-6424
North Carolina	Bill Hobbs	(919) 873-2061
North Dakota	Barry Borstad	(701) 250-4771
Ohio	Jerry Greenbaum	(614) 469-6744
Oklahoma	Mike Schrammel	(405) 742-1070
Oregon	Debbie Nichols	(503) 414-3337
Pennsylvania	Frank Wetherhold	(717) 782-4567
Puerto Rico	Johnny Hernandez	(787) 766-5095
South Carolina	Eva Franklin	(803) 765-5884
South Dakota	Roger Hazuka	(605) 352-1132
Tennessee	Rickey Hickman	(615) 783-1375
Texas	Scooter Brockette	(817) 298-1305
Utah	Kimball Harward	(801) 524-3240 ext 129

Appendix E — Rural Housing Services State Offices (continued)

Vermont, New Hampshire, Virgin Islands	Mike Keller	(802) 828-6020
Virginia	Michelle C. Corridon	(804) 287-1595
Washington	Clint Kaasa	(509) 664-0220
West Virginia	Scott Mullins	(304) 263-6495
Wisconsin	Paul Bartlett	(715) 345-7670
Wyoming	John Johnson	(307) 261-6315

Appendix F
Federal Home Loan Banks

Federal Home Loan Bank of Boston
One Financial Center 20th floor
Boston, MA 02110
(617) 542-0150

Federal Home Loan of New York
7 World Trade Center, Floor 22
New York, NY 10048-1185
(212) 441-6600

Federal Home Loan Bank of Pittsburgh
601 Grant Street
Pittsburgh, PA 15219-4455
(412) 288-7316

Federal Home Loan Bank of Atlanta
1475 Peachtree Street NE
Atlanta, GA 30309
(404) 888-8435

Federal Home Loan Bank of Cincinnati
221 E. Fourth St., Atrium Two
Cincinnati, OH 45202
(513) 852-7615

Federal Home Loan Bank
of San Francisco, P.O.Box 7948
San Francisco, CA 94120
(415) 616-2749

Federal Home Loan Bank of Chicago
111 East Wacker Drive, Suite 800
One Financial Center, 20th floor
Chicago, IL 60601
(312) 565-5700

Federal Home Loan Bank of Indianapolis
8250 Woodfield Blvd.
Indianapolis, IN 46240
(317) 465-0428

Federal Home Loan Bank of Des Moines
907 Walnut Street
Des Moines, IA 50309
(515) 281-1109

Federal Home Loan Bank of Dallas
5605 N. MacArthur Blvd, 9th floor
Irving, TX 75038
(214) 714-8647

Federal Home Loan Bank of Topeka
120 East 6th Street, 2 Townsite Plaza
Topeka, KS 66603
(913) 233-0507 x565

Federal Home Loan Bank of San Francisco
307 East Chapman Avenue
Orange, CA 92666-1507
(714) 633-1271

Federal Home Loan Bank of Seattle
1501 4th Avenue, 19th Floor
Seattle, WA 98101-1693
(206)340-2300

Appendix G
Fannie Mae Offices

Home Office:

Fannie Mae
Native American Housing Initiatives
3900 Wisconsin Avenue, NW
Washington, D.C. 20016
(202) 752-7407

Regional Offices:

Atlanta, GA	(404) 398-6054
Chicago, IL	(312) 368-6200
Dallas, TX	(214) 773-7659
Pasadena, CA	(818) 396-5140
Philadelphia, PA	(215) 575-1400

Lender:

Sound Development Association (206) 426-4641